THE BALVIHAR BOOK OF TRAIN THE BRAIN

Illustrations by

Bharati Sukhatankar

CENTRAL CHINMAYA MISSION TRUST
MUMBAI - 400 072

© **Central Chinmaya Mission Trust**

First Edition	December	- 2001	- 3,000 copies
Reprint	May	- 2002	- 2,000 copies
Reprint	February	- 2003	- 2,000 copies
Reprint	October	- 2004	- 2,000 copies
Reprint	November	- 2005	- 2,000 copies
Reprint	January	- 2007	- 2,000 copies
Reprint	February	- 2009	- 3,000 copies

Published by:
Central Chinmaya Mission Trust
Sandeepany Sadhanalaya
Saki Vihar Road,
Mumbai-400 072. India,
Tel.: 091-22-2857 2367, 2857 5806
Fax : 091-22-2857 3065
Email :ccmt@chinmayamission.com
Website: www.chinmayamission.com

Distribution Centre in USA:
Chinmaya Mission West
Publications Dicision
560 Bridgetown Pike,
Langhorne, PA 19053, USA
Tel.: (215) 396-0390
Fax: (215) 396-9710
www. chinmayapublicatons.org
publications@chinmaya.org

Printed by:
JAK Printers Pvt. Ltd.,
JAK Compound,
Dadoji Konddeo Cross Lane,
Off. Dr. Babasaheb Ambedkar Marg,
Byculla (East), Mumbai - 400 027.
Tel.: 2377 2222 Telefax: 2377 1212
Email: jakprint@vsnl.com

Price: Rs. 100.00

ISBN: 978-81-7597-024-3

Foreword

The Bal Vihar magazine has played a vital role in the history of the Chinmaya Mission. Started in 1969 by Pujya Gurudev Swami Chinmayananda it was aimed at moulding the minds of the children and thereby laying the foundation for producing men and women of strong moral character, upholding the timeless values of Indian culture. Pujya Gurudev's idea was to "catch them young."

Towards this goal, Bal Vihar has worked for over thirty years. Much valuable material has been published so far and so it was decided that in this, the 50th year of the Chinmaya Movement, it would be a good idea to reprint a series of all-colour Bal Vihar books under different titles. This would strengthen the grass root level activities and help the Bal Vihar children and sevaks.

I commend the work done by the Bal Vihar team and wish them all success in their ongoing efforts.

Mumbai

December 2001

(Swami Tejomayanada)

EDITOR'S NOTE

Train the Brain has been a regular feature of Bal Vihar since 1996.

This selected offering of Teasers and Puzzles is brought out as a tribute to our beloved Gurudev, Swami Chinmayananda, in this, the 50th year of the Chinmaya Movement.

(Brni. Vividisa Chaitanya)

Mumbai

December 2001

FIGURE IT OUT.....

1. In a paved yard, some boys were playing with a small ball. There was a hole in the yard, and the ball rolled into it. The hole was about a meter in depth but barely bigger than the ball in diameter. The

boys were dismayed at losing their ball – till one of them had a bright idea. Soon they were playing as before – and they didn't even bother to cover the hole. What did they do?

2. Mr. Kumar told the following story :
We put a nesting box in our garden and it caused a tragedy. A pair of titmice laid their eggs there but when they were absent to get food, a cuckoo

came and laid its egg among the others. All the eggs were hatched by the titmice. However, when the young cuckoo had grown, it was too big to

leave the box and so it died. What do you have to say?

3. A bus has 5 stops. It carries 60 passengers. At the first stop, 15 get down, at the second stop, 3 get down. At the third stop, half the passengers get down and 10 at the fourth stop. How many people get down at the last stop?

4. 12 carpenters take 8 days to finish a piece of work. If 4 more carpenters are brought in, how many days will it take?

5. Tiger is a ferocious bulldog, tied to a tree with a long rope. He does not allow anyone to come anywhere near him. While playing, your football ends up near the tree. How will you retrieve your football?

TAKE TWO MINUTES...

6. This box contains numbers 1 to 9 several times. Only two numbers are given twice. Which are they? What is the total of all the numbers in the box?

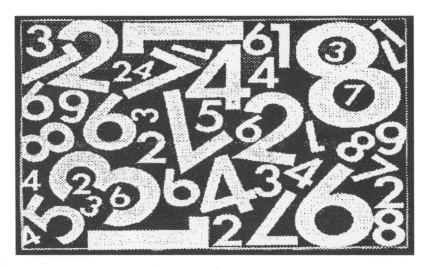

7. Which of the 5 dark figures fits exactly into the white figure?

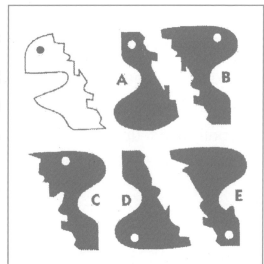

8. Examine the figure carefully and answer the following questions.
a) How many triangles are there?
b) How many rectangles can you find?
c) How many hexagons do you see?

9. How many cubes have been used to build each of these figures?

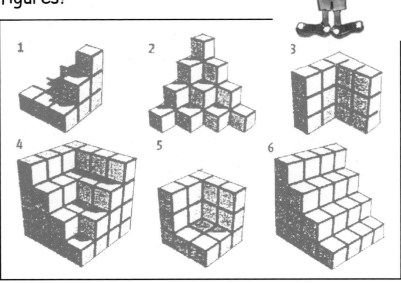

10. Each string joins one number with one letter. Find out which number connects which letter. You are allowed to pursue the string only with your eyes.

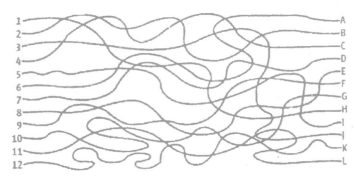

11. Which two butterflies are identical?

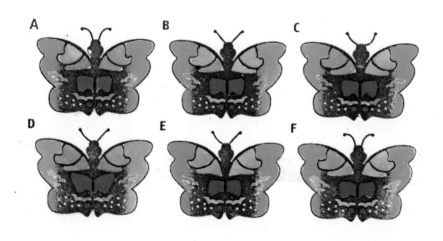

12. This triangle is formed with 7 matchsticks.

Without adding or taking away any matchstick, form 3 triangles out of them.

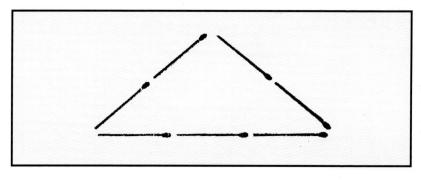

13. Ten coins have been used to form a triangle pointing upwards. Move only 3 coins to form a triangle pointing downwards

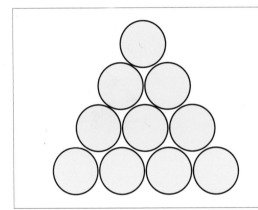

ARITHMETRICK

14. A certain number, when divided by 7, 5 remains. The same when divided by 9, then 7 remains. What is the number?

Hint : Multiply the two dividing numbers and substract from the sum, the difference between the dividing numbers.

15. Answer quickly, do not use pen or pencil. Which sum is greater, that of the figures on the left or on the right?

987654321	123456789
87654321	12345678
7654321	1234567
654321	123456
54321	12345
4321	1234
321	123
21	12
1	1

ALL IN THE FAMILY

16. Kamala said to Veena, "Your brother's wife's mother-in-law is my grandmother." What is Kamala's relatiohship with Veena?

17. Raghav introduced a girl thus, "This girl's mother is my mother-in-law's only daughter." How is Raghav related to the girl?

18. Wamanrao said, "This lady's father-in-law is the father of the person whose

father-in-law is my father." How is Wamanrao related to the lady?

19. DEVELOP THIS : Which of the five photos was made from the negative?

20. If you pull each rope at both ends, which ones will have a knot?

QUICK ONES

21. Name a way no one ever uses.

22. When does a Chinaman say "Good Bye"?

23. Which question can never be answered with "Yes".

24

Sukhram's peacock wandered into Maniram's farm and laid an egg there. Who is the rightful owner of the egg? Sukhram or Maniram?

25.

Look at these faces. Two in each row are alike. One is different in one detail. Which?

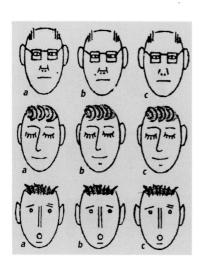

26.

From 1-10 are shapes which, when brought together, will form one of the shapes from 'a-e'. No gaps to remain in between and no edges to jut out. For instance, '1-c'. i.e. when you put the pieces of '1' together, you get 'c'. Now can you do the others?

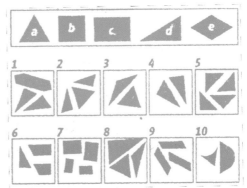

27. What should the missing figures look like?

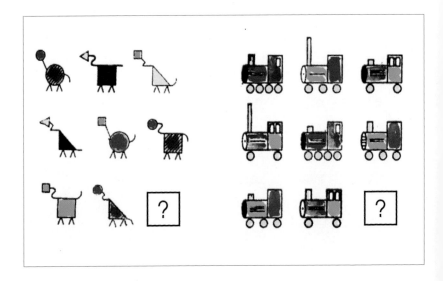

FLEX THOSE GREY CELLS

28. A farmer was asked how many animals he had on his farm. He replied, "They are all horses but two, all sheep but two, and all pigs but two." How many animals did he have in all?

29. If a turkey weighs 10 Kg. and a half of its own weight, what does the turkey weigh?

30. Using just 3 digits, write out a simple addition sum that totals 24. The digits must all be the same, but you cannnot use 8!

31. Last night, the police arrested a stranger in a hotel. Next morning, a guest recounted the story. "I was going to bed, when someone knocked on my door. When I opened it, a man was in the hallway. He said he was sorry, he thought that was his room. I knew at once that he was a thief, called the police and had him arrested." A lady asked, "But how did you know he intended to steal?" Well how?

32. Put 8 number 8s in such a position that they will result in 1,000.

33. Pran was travelling by car when he got into a terrible thunderstorm. He came to a crossroad where he found the storm had blown down the sign post. Now he was confused – which road should he take? Suddenly, he knew. He put the signpost back in place and reached his destination correctly. How did he help himself?

34. Three boys discovered a cave and went in to explore it. Suddenly, there were rushing sounds above their heads and the boy holding the torch dropped it. Now all was pitch dark. Another boy had a box of matches. Considering that one match burns for 15 seconds and it took them 15 minutes to reach the exit, how many matches did they need?

35. Three Friends. Which of the cutouts corresponds to the original photo?

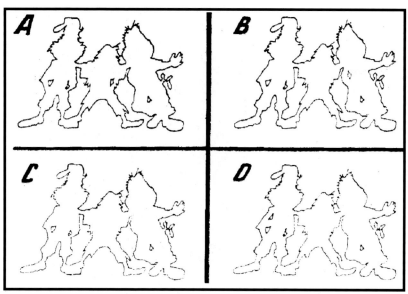

36. Which two are exactly alike?

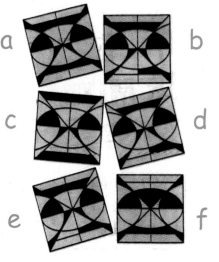

37.

How many snakes?

38.

A king was angry with his astrologer and said, "If you are so smart, tell the date of your death, or I'll kill you." The astrologer said, "The stars never lie and I know their secrets. I will tell you when I have to die..." What did the astrologer say to avoid being killed?

39. A wine merchant when he died, left his 3 sons, 7 full, 7 half full and 7 empty barrels and said that each son should inherit the same number of full, half full and empty barrels. How was this done?

40. Yesterday it was 5 days to Sunday. Which day is tomorrow? (Aid: count 5 days back from Sunday that was 'yesterday'. The day after it is 'today' and the next day is 'tomorrow'.

41. Find the correct rhythm – 5 4 8 7 14 13 26?

42. With a box before him, he defeats many an opponent. Who is he?

43. Write the number 42 in two different ways, each time using the same 3 numbers.

44. On board a large ship, a news bulletin was printed daily. It reported all the events on board. Recently a strange death was described : "One of our passengers, Choudhary Sher Singh, was having an afternoon nap on the upper deck. He dreamt of being chased by a ferocious tiger. Trying to run away, he leapt from his chair and  ran to the railing. In his panic, he jumped overboard and drowned."

Good reporting but something seems wrong. What?

45.
Which path will Hari, the Hammer have to take to hit Nitin, the Nail on the head.

THE WONDERFUL WAY OF WORDS

46. Quiz The Asses

a) The 'ass' that helps –

b) The 'ass' that talks with certainty –

c) The 'ass' that thinks on its own –

d) A group of 'asses' –

e) The 'asses' that gather at one place –

f) The 'ass' that kills –

g) The competent 'ass' -

h) The 'ass' that attacks –

i) The 'ass' that absorbs –

j) The 'ass' that agrees –

47. A BOXING MATCH

Here are 12 boxes and their 12 users. You have to match them correctly.

Time limit: 2 minutes

1) Sand box   panelist

2) Mail box   writer

3) Soap box   bandit

4) Jury box   angler

5) Shoe box   voter

6) Press box   gardener

7) Hat box   realtor

8) Tackle box   toddler

9) Flower box   postman

10) Salt box   orator

11) Strong box   cobbler

12) Ballot box   milliner

48. What is the connection between the following words? Three are given, find the fourth. For example, Dog is to kennel as horse is to shed.

Now try these:

1) Desert is to sand as _____ is to water.

2) Candle is to flame as lamp is to _____.

3) Water is to ice as dew is to _____.

4) Lungs are to humans as _____ are to fish.

5) Key is to piano as _____ is to violin.

6) Chain is to _____ as house is to room.

7) Words are to language as _____ are to alphabet.

8) Book is to paper as painting is to _____.

9) Parliament is to democracy as king is to _____.

10) Day is to morning as _____ is to evening.

11) Wood is to table as _____ is to pot.

12) Wool is to lamb as silk is to _____.

13) Song is to bird as _____ is to lion.

14) Firmness is to rock as _____ is to water.

15) Lawyer is to court as _____ is to hospital.

49. There are many animals in this farmyard. One animal is hiding which does not belong. Can you find it?

50. The hunter is scared of the leopard. Can you find it?

MAGIC SQUARES

A magic square is generally a chess board figure in which numbers are so arranged that the sum of digits, no matter in which direction they are added, is always the same. One of the main sources of the magic square is GANITA KAUMUDI, a mathematical treatise written in AD 1356. In this book, an entire chapter discusses the construction of these squares, with either an odd or even number of cells.

Some magic squares are said to posses mystical properties. Given below is one such square. It is the simplest type of magic square and based on the magic power of the number 15, is said to be all-beneficent. Numbers from 1-9 are placed in a specified order in the nine squares, of which four squares represent the elements. To cure cold, the

FIRE

AIR

8	3	4
1	5	9
6	7	2

EARTH

WATER

numbers are written beginning with 1, clockwise from the 'fire' square; to cure fever, from the 'water' square, to effect the speedy return of a person from a distant land, from the 'air' square. The book advises that the magic square be drawn on paper with sandalwood or saffron and for an unfailingly beneficial effect, be worn as an amulet!

51. Complete the magic square using the missing numbers (from 1-16) 13, 14, 15 and 16, in such a way that whichever way you read it - vertically, horizantally or diagonally, each row will total 34.

Also, the numbers in the four corners will total 34 as also a number of adjacent clusters of four!

10	8	1	15
3	13	12	6
16	2	7	9
5	11	14	4

52. Write missing odd numbers from 3-19 in the blank squares in such a way that across, down and diagonally, the squares add up to 33.

- Do not move 3, 5 and 7

- Each number will appear only once in one square.

- Start! You have only 2 minutes to crack this one.

53.

Only one object appears in both pictures. Can you tell which one?

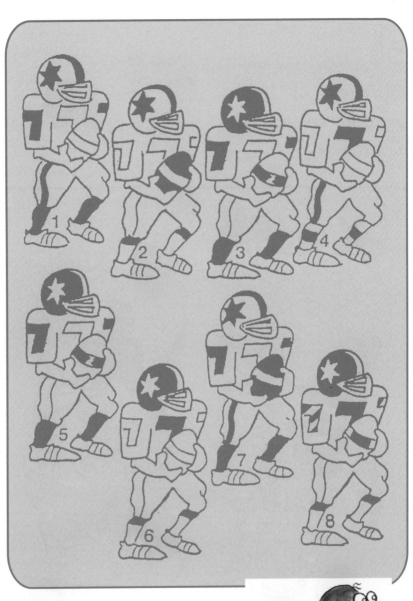

54. Two of these eight football players are the same. Which?

55. Where are the hunter and his dog hiding? Colour the picture.

56. Here are six different pictures. One contains one object each from each of the other pictures. What is the number of that picture?

WEAR YOUR THINKING CAP....

57. The quiz master presented a hundred rupee note to a participant and said, "It is yours if you can express the value of this note in three dissimilar ways without using zeros. You have 10 seconds for the answer."

58. Two mountaineers were climbing a high mountain when one of them shortly before reaching the peak, fell and hurt himself. The other one continued without minding his friend. When the second fellow too reached the peak, he was angry and looked in the opposite direciton. Without turning his face, the first fellow said, "Your nose is bleeding." How did he know?

59. A man wakes up in the middle of the night and remembers suddenly that he does not have to get up at 5 O'clock, but at 4 O'clock. The electricity is off, he has no matches or torch. His alarm has a luminous dial, but the hour hand is not visible. He doesn't have neighbours and doesn't want to miss his sleep. The alarm has to go off one hour earlier, but how?

60. Rabbits and chicks -both are kept together in a cage. The count is 35 heads and 94 legs. How many rabbits and how many chicks in the cage?

61. There are about 9000 books written about Napoleon. A new one was published recently in which it was said that Napoleon was admitted to the Military Academy of Brienne. He was said to have enjoyed his duties, cleaned his weapons himself. In his spare time, he liked to play with his friends with a toy railroad train but did not like dolls or tin soldiers. True?

62. If it costs one rupee to break a link and two rupees to weld it again, what is the least it would cost to join in a single length of chain, the five segments shown here?
Twelve Rupees? Try again. The correct answer is less.
Remember, the most obvious way is not always the most economical.

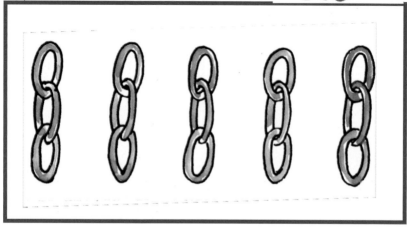

63.

Tojo hates taking a bath Mandy loves giving it to him!

Find 8 differences in the two pictures.

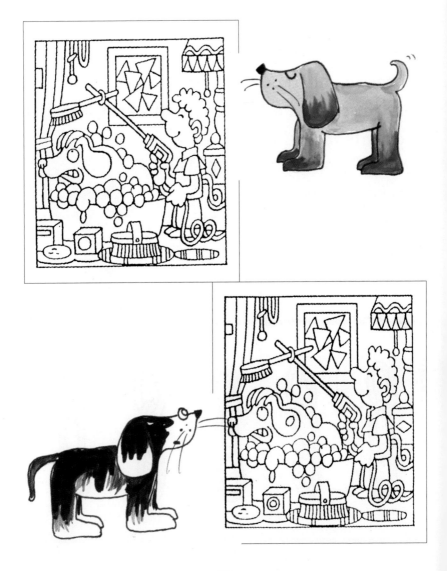

BE QUICK!...

64. Which word is spelled wrong in all the dictionaries?

65. What do we call creatures with four legs, which fly?

66. A farmer had 17 sheep. All but 9 escaped through a hole in the fence. How many remained?

67. Prof. Rao can make five equal parts using three lines only. Can you?

GLOBALLY

Here are some riddles for you and they have come from different parts of the world. Can you figure out the answers? Try.

68. From America – Two bodies have I, though joined in one; the stiller I stand, the faster I run.

69. From Mexico – White as the snow, black as the coal, she walks and has no feet, she speaks and has no mouth.

70. From Lithuania – What lives without a body, speaks without a tongue, everyone can hear it, yet no one can see it?

71. From Iceland – I am found to be swifter than fire or wind. I travel to unknown worlds which mortal eye has never seen and change them around in the twinkling of an eye.

72. From England – The beginning of eternity, the end of time and space, the  beginning of every end, and the end of every place.

73. From Spain – It conquers the lion, it conquers the tiger and it conquers the enraged bull; it conquers men and kings. They all fall, overcome, at its feet.

74. Here are three figures. You have to piece them together so that they form a 'pyramid' (shape of a triangle)

Hint : Trace out these figures on a piece of

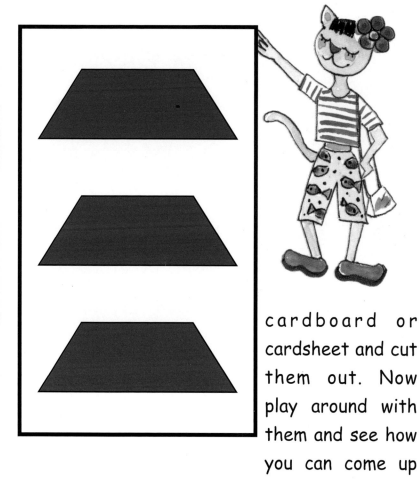

cardboard or cardsheet and cut them out. Now play around with them and see how you can come up

with the required figure.

75. Colour this picture of Tropical Fish. Then find out, how many?

76. Radha walked into the garden and found some toadstools. Can you help her count how many?

THINK QUICK!

77. A scooter driver ran over a chicken and killed it. The owner wanted Rs.50/- for it. The driver didn't want to pay – he did not eat meat and had no use for a dead chicken. He was willing to pay Rs.25/-, but the owner did not agree. So they argued, until a postman came along and quickly found a solution acceptable to all. How?

78. Without using pencil and paper, can you tell which result is higher   that of 1+2+3+4 or 1x2x3x0x5?

79. Chintu was caught by cannibals who were about to eat him. The cannibal chief said, " I will give you one chance. In this pot are two chits – one says, "I live" and the other says, "I die". Pick one, and it shall decide your fate.

Now Chintu had already overheard two tribals discussing that both chits had, "I die" written on them. Whichever chit Chintu picked, death was certain. How did Chintu escape from his awful fate?

80. What is the figure that should go in the third box?

81. THE GREAT ESCAPE

The lion has escaped
from the cage.
Where is it hiding?

No. KNOW ALL!

82. Do you like fooling your friends with numbers? Try this on them.

- Write a number on a piece of paper, put it inside an envelope and seal it.

- Ask your friend to think of any 3-digit number in which all three digits are the same, i.e. 111, 222, 333, 444, 555, etc. upto 999.

- Now ask him to add up the numbers of the digits. eg. 1+1+1=3, or 4+4+4=12 or 9+9+9=27.

- Ask him to divide the original 3-digit number by the sum of the 3-digits i.e. 111 , by 3 or 444 , by 12 or 999 , by 27.

- Ask him to give you the answer.

- It will always be 37!

(And of course, 37 is the number you have written on the piece of paper in the sealed envelope!)

83. Tell your friend that 100 + 11 makes 199

- He will say, no, it doesn't. It makes 111.
- Your friend gets angry and says, prove it!
- Here's what you do -

$$100 + 11 = 199$$

QUICK!

84. How many fishes are there in the barrel?

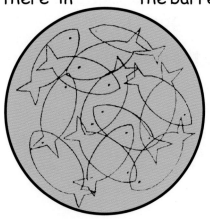

85. Which photo is made from the negative on top?

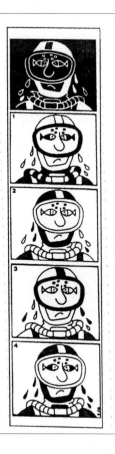

86. Which two rows are the same?

87. Which line is longer, the vertical or the horizontal?

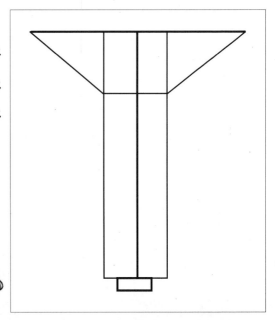

88. Murli has lost his key. Can you help him find it? The key you find should be exactly the same as the one in the box.

89. Oh dear, somebody lost his marbles. How many?

60–160–260–360?

NOW COLOUR THE PICTURE

90. One of the cubes 1 - 6 is missing in Block A and one in Block B. Which one?

No. KNOW ALL AGAIN!

91. Choose any number between 1 and 9, multiply it by 11. Multiply the result by 9091 - Voila! Your original number appears as the first and the last number of the final result!

92. Would you believe it, there are times when multiplication can equal division! Doesn't make much sense?

a) If you have to divide a number by 0.5, try multiplying it by 2 instead - you'll get the same answer!

e.g.: $10 \div 0.5 = 20$ and $10 \times 2 = 20$, which is easier to do?

b) If you have to divide a number by 0.25, try multiplying it by 4 instead - you'll get the same answer.

e.g.: $20 \div 0.25 = 80$ and $20 \times 4 = 80$, Got it?

c) Now, a number to be divided by 0.125, can be multiplied by 8 to get the same answer!

e.g.: $30 \div 0.125 = 240$ and $30 \times 8 = 240$

d) Take a number like 6, 835, 916, 547, 995 - won't it be easier to multiply it by 2 than to divide by 0.5?

93. Find out the six differences in the mirror image of the picture.

94. A man owned ten horses. But he had a stable which could only accommodate nine horses, one in each section. How did he put ten horses in his stable.

95. How many things can you find in the picture that start with "B"? 30? Time : 30 seconds.

DOUBLE DELIGHT!

96. There are three rows of clues for the three rows of answers. The first clue gives a 5-letter word, four letters of the word make up the answer to the second clue and three letters of that make up the word to the third clue. The unused letters are entered in Column 'A' and Column 'B' respectively. When the entire lot of clues are answered, the letters in the columns give the names of two wars in Indian History.

Express by words	Green vegetable	Expanse of water
Animal	Shopping plaza	Scooter Company (Vespa)
Purify	Stick	First in a pack of cards
Pertaining to a charged particle	Not paper money	Cheat
Monkey trick	Place of amusement	Noah's boat
Rank	Challenge	Colour
Rubbish	Direction	Stitch

97. One of the following words does not logically fit in with the others. Which?

Dhow, yacht, sloop, hansom, cutter, steamer, freighter, cruiser?

98. Two fathers and two sons go to a restaurant, eat one pizza each. On leaving, they pay for 3 pizzas and the waiter is satisfied. How come?

99. 2 candles are burning, both of same length and thickness. One made from tallow, the other from wax. Which candle burns longer?

100. Which is the smallest number you can write using 2 numbers?

101. A visitor was astonished at the number of books in the professor's library. The professor said, "and 125 books are not even here, the 20th part is lent out, a 30th part is in another room". How many books does the professor have?

102. Grandfather recently had a birthday. Manu made a drawing of his, using numbers. If you add up these numbers, you will discover grandfather's age.

103.

Which piece fits the broken picture?

ANSWERS

1. They put water into the hole which made the ball rise to the surface.

2. If the hole in the box was big enough for the mother cuckoo to come in, it would be big enough for the fledgling to fly out.

3. 13 people get down at the last stop.
   [15+3+21+10 = 49. 60 – 49 = 11 passengers + driver + cleaner = 13].

4. 12 carpenters take 8 days. So, 16 carpenters will take 6 days.
   [12x8/16]

5. First, stand in front of the dog, at a safe distance. Then start running round the tree. The dog will run after you. Take several rounds of the tree - his rope will get shorter with each round. A point will come when you can retrieve your football without being snapped at by Tiger.

6. 5 and 9 are given twice. The total is 205.

7. Figure B.

8. a-14 ; b-7 ; c-2

9. 1-13 ; 2-20 ; 3-15 ; 4-50 ; 5-19 ; 6-40

10. 1- H ; 2- B ; 3- J ; 4- C ; 5 - I ; 6 - A ; 7 - D ; 8 - E ; 9 - F ; 10 - G ; 11- L; 12- K.

11. A and F .

12.

13. Move the topmost coin below the lowest row. Then take the 2 outer coins from this row and move them upward to the 2nd row from top.

14. 61 [{7x9}- 2]

15. Believe it or not, they both add up to the same - 1,083,676, 269

16. Veena is Kamala's aunt {father's sister}

17. She is his daughter.

18 Wamanrao is the lady's brother.

19 . 5.

20. 2 and 3.

21. The Milky Way.

22. When he knows English.

23 Are you asleep ?

24. Neither Sukhram nor Maniram. Peacocks are male and do not lay eggs.

25. First Row - c - nose ; Second Row -a - chin; Third Row - b - eyebrow.

26. 1 -c, 2-e, 3-d, 4-a, 5-b, 6-d, 7-b, 8-c, 9-e, 10-a .

27.

28. 3

29. 20 Kg.

30. 22+2=24

31. If it was the thief's room, why would he knock on the door?

32. 888+88+8+8+8=1,000

33. Pran knew from WHERE he was travelling and the direction in which his car was. So he put the sign-post in such a way that one arm pointed to the name and direction from WHERE he came. Then he knew how to go on.

33. Pran knew from WHERE he was travelling and the direction in which his car was. So he put the sign-post in such a way that one arm pointed to the name and direction from WHERE he came. Then he knew how to go on.

34. They needed just one match to find the torch.

35. C

36. b and e

37. 6

38. The astrologer said, "My death will be exactly 24hrs before yours." So if the King wanted to live, he also had to allow his astrologer to live.

39. Pour 4 of the half - filled barrels to make 2 full ones. Then you get 9 full, 3 half - full and 9 empty.

40. Thursday   **41.**   25

42. A boxer.   **43.**   6 x 6 + 6;   7 x 7 - 7

44. How did the reporter know what the passenger was dreaming?

45. Three

46. (a) Assist (b) Assert (c) Assume (d) Association
(e) Assemble (f) Assassinate (g) Asset (h) Assault
(i) Assimilate (j) Assent.

47. 1) toddler 2) postman 3) orator 4) panelist 5) cobbler
6) writer 7) milliner 8) angler 9) gardener 10) realtor
11) bandit 12) voter

48. 1) Ocean 2) Bulb 3) Frost 4) Gills 5) String 6) Link
7) Letters 8) Canvas 9) Monarchy 10) Night 11) Mud
12) Worm 13) Roar 14) Flow 15) Doctor

49. Turn the picture upside down. The penguin is hiding in the tree.

50. Bottom centre - turn the picture upside down for a better view!

51.

10	8	1	15
3	13	12	6
16	2	7	9
5	11	14	4

52.

5	15	13
19	11	3
9	7	17

53.   The nail appears in both the pictures.

54.   3 and 5

55.   Hunter - E 2/3, Dog - A2

56.   No. 3 — It has the fence from No. 1, the house from No. 2, the pig from No. 4, the nest from No. 5 and the cloud from No. 6.

57.   1 - 99 + 1; 2 - Roman C; 3 - HUNDRED

58.   The two were facing each other, one looking east, the other west, so they could see each other's face.

59.   He advances the minute hand by one hour.

60.   12 rabbits and 23 chicks.

61.   False. At that time there were no rail roads or toy trains.

62.   Nine Rupees. Take the first group of 3 links and break each one. (Cost is three rupees). Then use each link to join two of the other groups (Cost for 3 welding jobs, six rupees).

63.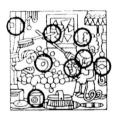

64.   WRONG

65.   Two birds

66.   Nine

67.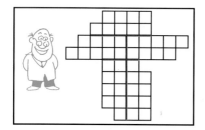

68. Hour Glass

69. A letter

70. Echo

71. Thought or dream

72. The letter 'E'

73. Sleep

74.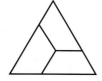

75. 20

76. 30

77. He took the Rs. 25/- from the driver, added Rs. 25/- from his own pocket, gave the money to the owner, and went home with a chicken cheaply bought!

78. The addition has a higher result (10) for any multiplication by 0 results in 0.

79. Chintu drew one chit and swallowed it. Since the other chit had "I die" on it, Chintu insisted that the swallowed chit had "I live" written on it.

80. Multiply diagonally opposite numbers and then add them to get the number in the square.
[2x4] + [5x3] = 23
[3x5] + [6x4] = 39
[4x6] + [7x5] = 59

81. It is hiding in the tree.

82. Heh! Heh!

83. Heh! Heh!

84. 13

85. No. 2

86. 2 and 7

87. They are of the same length.

88. B

89. 260

90. A - 5, B -1

91. Heh! Heh!

92. Heh! Heh!

93.

94.

T	E	N	H	O	R	S	E	S

95. Beetles, bag, bicycle, banyan, branches, bird, boy, braces, boots, belt, buckle, bushes, basket, bottle, bracelet, bonnet, braids, blouse, barefeet, bud, butterfly, bee, box, bucket, brush, bowl, bananas, barn, bell, balloons.

blouse, barefeet, bud, butterfly, bee, box, bucket, brush, bowl, bananas, barn, bell, balloons.

96.

1)	SPEAK	(K)	PEAS (P)	SEA
2)	LLAMA	(A)	MALL (A)	LML
3)	CLEAN	(L)	CANE (N)	ACE
4)	IONIC	(I)	COIN (I)	CON
5)	PRANK	(N)	PARK (P)	ARK
6)	GRADE	(G)	DARE (A)	RED
7)	WASTE	(A)	WEST (T)	SEW

97. Hansom

98. They were only 3 - grandpa, father and son.

99. Neither. Both will burn shorter.

100. One, if written as a fraction 1/1

101. 1,500

102. 61 years

Cover Page Answers

1. 33 Triangles

2.

2	9	4
7	5	3
6	1	8

3.